It's a Dragonfly!

Elisa Peters

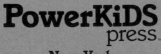
PowerKiDS
press™
New York

For Jean Leng

Published in 2009 by The Rosen Publishing Group, Inc.
29 East 21st Street, New York, NY 10010

First Edition

Editor: Amelie von Zumbusch
Book Design: Greg Tucker
Photo Researcher: Jessica Gerweck

Photo Credits: All images by Shutterstock.com.

Library of Congress Cataloging-in-Publication Data

Peters, Elisa.
  It's a dragonfly! / Elisa Peters.
       p. cm. — (Everyday wonders)
  Includes index.
  ISBN 978-1-4042-4460-3 (library binding)
  1. Dragonflies—Juvenile literature. I. Title.
  QL520.P48 2009
  595.7'33—dc22

                                          2007046333

Manufactured in the United States of America

Contents

Dragonflies are beautiful bugs.

⑤

Dragonflies come in many colors. Some are red.

Other dragonflies are gold.

All dragonflies have two pairs of **wings**.

11

Dragonflies have a long body.

Each dragonfly has a pair of strange-looking **eyes**.

Young dragonflies are called **nymphs**.

Nymphs **shed** their skin before becoming adult dragonflies.

Dragonflies almost always live near water.

Dragonflies feed on flies and other bugs.

23

Words to Know

eyes

nymph

shed

wings

Index

Web Sites

Due to the changing nature of Internet links, PowerKids Press has developed an online list of Web sites related to the subject of this book. This site is updated regularly. Please use this link to access the list:
www.powerkidslinks.com/wonder/dragonfly/